IMAGINE YOU WERE THERE...

# WINNING the VOTE for WOMEN

SUFFRAGETTE

DEEDS NOT WORDS

IMAGINE YOU WERE THERE...

# WINNING the VOTE for WOMEN

## CARYN JENNER

KINGFISHER
LONDON & NEW YORK

## KINGFISHER
### LONDON & NEW YORK

Copyright © Macmillan Publishers
International Ltd. 2019
Published in the United States by Kingfisher,
175 Fifth Ave., New York, NY 10010
Kingfisher is an imprint of Macmillan
Children's Books, London
All rights reserved.

Distributed in the U.S. and Canada by Macmillan,
175 Fifth Ave., New York, NY 10010
Library of Congress Cataloging-in-Publication data has been applied for.

Series editor: Elizabeth Yeates
Illustrations: Marc Pattenden (Advocate Art Agency)
Design: Dan Newman
Cover design: Laura Hall and Suzanne Cooper
Consultant: Professor Emerita June Purvis

ISBN: 978-0-7534-7501-0

Copyright © Macmillan Publishers International Ltd 2019

9 8 7 6 5 4 3 2 1
1TR/0319/WKT/UG/128MA

A CIP catalogue record for this book is available from the British Library.

Kingfisher books are available for special promotions and premiums. For
details contact: Special Markets Department, Macmillan, 175 Fifth Ave., New
York, NY 10010. For more information, please visit: www.kingfisherbooks.com
Printed in China

Picture credits: 7 GL Archive/Alamy Stock Photo; 8t Everett Historical/Shutterstock;
8b Lisa S./Shutterstock; 10 Everett Historical/Shutterstock; 11 Pictorial Press Ltd/
Alamy Stock Photo; 12l Everett Historical/Shutterstock; 12r Everett Historical/
Shutterstock; 12bl Chronicle/Alamy Stock Photo; 15tl Everett Historical/Shutterstock;
15r Everett Historical/Shutterstock; 15bl Everett Historical/Shutterstock; 18tr Everett
Historical/Shutterstock; 18l Everett Historical/Shutterstock; 18b Everett Historical/
Shutterstock; 19t Everett Historical/Shutterstock; 19r Pictorial Press Ltd / Alamy Stock
Photo; 20 History and Art Collection/Alamy Stock Photo; 21tr UtCon Collection/Alamy
Stock Photo; 21tl Everett Collection Historical/Alamy Stock Photo; 21cr Rapp Halour/Alamy
Stock Photo; 21cl 914 Collection/Alamy Stock Photo; 26 Pictorial Press Ltd/Alamy Stock
Photo; p28 Topical Press Agency/Stringer/Getty; p29 Manchester Daily Express/Getty;
31l Topical Press Agency/Getty; 31b Independent News and Media/Getty; 32r PhotoQuest/
Contributor/Getty; 32b Everett Historical/Shutterstock; 33 Fox Photos/Getty; 34 Pictoral
Press Ltd/Alamy Stock Photo; 36tr Bettmann/Getty; 36b Everett Historical/Shutterstock;
38 The History Collection/Alamy Stock Photo; 39 Library of Congress 3C05415; 40l Everett
Historical/Shutterstock; 40b Everett Historical/Shutterstock; 41 all Everett Historical/
Shutterstock; 42 Photo 12/Getty; 43 Sankei/Getty; 44l Bettmann/Getty; 45 Imagno/
Getty; 46 GL Archive/Alamy Stock Photo; 47 Fotografía de Kena Lorenzini donada al Museo de
la Memoria y los Derechos Humanos; 49 Everett Collection Historical/Alamy Stock Photo; 50r
AWAD AWAD/Getty; 50b Kdonmuang/Shutterstock; 54tr INTERFOTO/Alamy Stock Photo;
54br Trinity Mirror/Mirrorpix/Alamy Stock Photo; 57t sadikgulec/istock; 57cr Photographee.
eu/Shutterstock; 58tr lev radin/Shutterstock; 58cl DLGimages/Shutterstock; 58b M. Stan
Reaves/Alamy Stock Photo; 59l BonezBoyz/Shutterstock; 59r Ink Drop/Shutterstock;
60tl Art Reserve/Alamy Stock Photo; 60tr IanDagnall Computing/Alamy Stock Photo; 60b
Everett Collection Historical/Alamy Stock Photo; 61tl The History Collection/Alamy Stock
Photo; 60tr age fotostock/Alamy Stock Photo; 61bl IanDagnall Computing/Alamy Stock Photo;
61br PACIFIC PRESS/Alamy Stock Photo

# Contents

An Example for the World 6

Why Is Voting Important? 8

Not Fair! 10

Seneca Falls 12

Steps Forward and
Steps Back 14

People Power—For! 16

People Power—Against! 18

Early Successes 20

Winning in Canada 22

Women of the Russian
Revolution 24

British Suffragists 26

British Suffragettes 28

Drastic Actions 30

Women in World War I 32

After World War I 34

Suffrage in the U.S. 36

More Global Success 38

Women in World War II 40

Opposite Sides of the
World 42

Poet and Protester 44

From Poverty to Power 46

The Lioness of Lasabi 48

Recent Struggles 50

Votes for Women! 52

The Fight for Women's
Rights 54

Toward Equality 56

Gender Equality and You 58

Hall of Fame 60

Glossary 62

Index 64

# An Example for the World

*In 1893, New Zealand made world history when many women campaigned for the right to vote—and won. Women in other parts of the world were also fighting for the right to vote.*

Kate Sheppard had sailed from Great Britain to live in New Zealand in the 1860s. She liked that New Zealand was a new country that seemed open to new ideas. Both boys and girls went to school, and women often worked alongside men. But women were not allowed to vote.

Kate believed that men and women should be treated equally, and the best way to achieve this was for women to have the vote. Many people felt this was a step too far, but Kate was determined to fight.

**Kate Sheppard:** "All that separates, whether of race, class, creed, or sex, is inhuman, and must be overcome."

⇩ Kate became one of the first women in the country to take up cycling, a new hobby sweeping the world.

Kate and other women traveled across the country to persuade people. In 1893, almost 32,000 women—nearly one-third of the country's population—signed a petition (a written request to the government) asking the New Zealand parliament for the right to vote. Parliament passed the women's suffrage bill (a law), and New Zealand became an example for the rest of the world.

## Maori women

*The 1893 women's suffrage bill included Maori women. Maori people had been living in New Zealand long before white settlers arrived from Europe. Campaigner Meri Te Tai Mangakāhia (above) argued that because many Maori women were landowners, they should be able to vote.*

POLLING STATION

NEW ZEALAND
1893
VOTE WON

# Why Is Voting Important?

**Voting is your chance to have a say on the laws of your country. It's a way of making your voice heard. For women, in particular, voting is an important step toward greater equality (being treated the same) with men.**

During an election, voters have a choice of people, called candidates, who are running for government offices. These are the people who will set policies and make laws. Voters choose the candidate who they think will best put forward their own opinions in both local, regional, and national government. There's no guarantee that the candidate you vote for will win the election, but at least you'll have tried.

But if you can't vote, it's harder to have your opinions taken seriously by people in government. Elected officials generally pay more attention to people who can vote them into office than to those who can't vote at all. That's why the right to vote is so important.

⇧ In the past, some women were able to vote in local elections, but they had to fight for the right to vote in national elections that affected their entire country.

## A woman's right

*This woman is in a voting booth, marking a box on her ballot paper to vote for her chosen candidate. Another word for having the vote is "suffrage." Women's suffrage means women having the right to vote. Suffragists are men and women who campaign for women to have the vote.*

⇨ Candidates tell people what they would try to achieve if elected to office.

# Not Fair!

*Traditionally, men and women had different roles in life. Men were more likely to have an education, earn money, and participate in the wider world, while women were expected to look after the family and home. Women's rights were very limited in every aspect of life. It wasn't fair!*

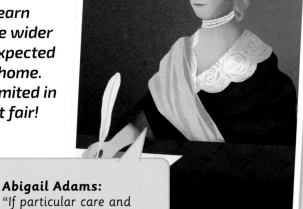

As far back as 1776, Abigail Adams campaigned for women's rights in a letter to her husband, John. He helped write the Declaration of Independence establishing the United States as a new nation that would make its own laws. John Adams would later become the second U.S. President.

**Abigail Adams:**
"If particular care and attention is not paid to the ladies, we are determined to foment a rebellion, and will not hold ourselves bound by any laws in which we have no voice or representation."

⇩ *Thomas Jefferson, Roger Sherman, Benjamin Franklin, Robert Livingston, and John Adams drafted the Declaration of Independence.*

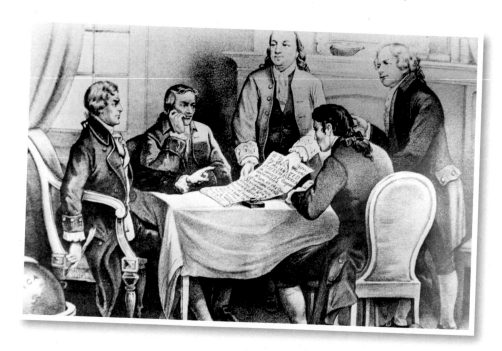

## Mary Wollstonecraft

*During the French Revolution (1789—1799), peasants fought for rights against the upper classes. Writer Mary Wollstonecraft supported the peasants, and insisted on more rights for women. In 1792, Wollstonecraft wrote, "I do not wish [women] to have power over men, but over themselves." Her essay influenced women's rights campaigners around the world.*

⇩ *In 1789, thousands of women marched to the French royal palace of Versailles to demand the king of France lower the price of bread so their families wouldn't starve.*

# Seneca Falls

*In 1848, the first Woman's Rights Convention took place in Seneca Falls, New York. It declared that "all men and women are created equal" and that women should legally have the right to vote, equal education, and equal treatment.*

Elizabeth Cady Stanton and Lucretia Mott met while campaigning against slavery. They organized the Woman's Rights Convention to discuss the rights of women in a variety of matters. About 300 people—mainly women—attended the historic convention. Newspapers claimed the convention was "insane and ludicrous" and "a monstrous injury to mankind."

But Stanton, Mott, and their supporters did not back down. They continued to campaign and inspired other suffragists around the world.

⇧ *Elizabeth Cady Stanton*

⇧ *Lucretia Mott*

**Susan B. Anthony:**
"Failure is impossible!"

## Supporters at Seneca Falls

*The Woman's Rights Convention featured many key speakers and campaigners, both men and women. Their inspirational speeches made people more determined to win the battle for equality.*

*Susan B. Anthony became an outspoken leader of the suffrage movement.*

*Frederick Douglass campaigned against slavery, and also participated in the Woman's Rights Convention.*

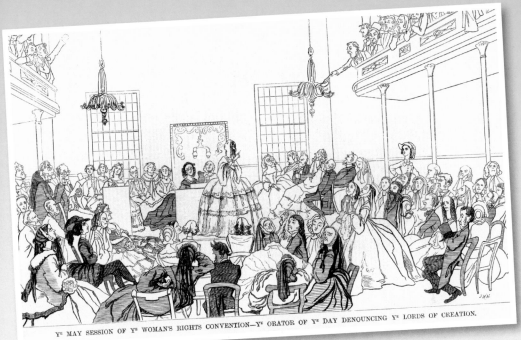

Yᴱ MAY SESSION OF Yᴱ WOMAN'S RIGHTS CONVENTION—Yᴱ ORATOR OF Yᴱ DAY DENOUNCING Yᴱ LORDS OF CREATION.

⇧ The Woman's Rights Convention was not taken seriously by newspapers. They published cartoons that mocked the event.

⇨ Statues of those who attended the Woman's Rights Convention can be seen in the Women's Rights Museum in Seneca Falls.

**Sojourner Truth:** "I could work as much and eat as much as a man."

Born a slave, Sojourner Truth made a speech in 1851 about the need for black women to have more rights.

Lucy Stone was a passionate speaker. She kept her own surname when she married.

Henry Stanton campaigned for both the abolition of slavery and women's rights.

Amelia Bloomer wore, balloon-style trousers under her skirt that became known as "bloomers."

# Steps Forward and Steps Back

As the population grew in the United States, so did opportunities for women to have a better education. Women's colleges opened a new world of learning, and more women began to question their traditional role in society. The events at Seneca Falls led to more conventions across the country.

⇩ Campaigns for female education were happening worldwide. In 1892, women were finally allowed to study at the University of Sydney in Australia.

↑ Dr. Mary Edwards Walker volunteered as a surgeon during the American Civil War (1861—1865). She was arrested as a spy and was held as a prisoner of war.

In 1865, slavery was abolished in the U.S., and a few years later, the 14th Amendment to the U.S. Constitution was intended to grant equality—except it referred only to men. In 1870, the 15th Amendment stated that "The right of citizens of the United States to vote shall not be denied . . . on account of race, color, or previous condition of servitude [slavery]." But the amendment did not mention a person's sex. It was a major setback for women's suffrage.

↑ Victoria Woodhull was the first female candidate for the office of U.S. president.

In 1869, the territory of Wyoming granted women the vote. Esther Morris, who had come to Wyoming from New York, was a follower of Susan B. Anthony. She suggested that giving women the vote would encourage more upstanding residents to make their homes in the territory, to balance out the cowboys, gamblers, and gold seekers. Wyoming became a U.S. state in 1890 and insisted on keeping women's suffrage. Within the next few years, other western states also granted women the vote. But the rest of the country was left behind.

⇦ Women's suffrage was won in Wyoming in 1869.

WYOMING
1869
VOTE WON

# People Power—For!

*Like the women of Seneca Falls, suffragists realized that people power was essential.*

**North America**

VOTES FOR WOMEN

EQUALITY FOR WOMEN

Campaigners were determined to have their voices heard and to spread their message around the world.

All over the world, suffragists came together to form organizations with a common goal: to win the vote for women.

As well as campaigning for women's rights, suffrage organizations also provided a safe forum for women to share their feelings of discontent. Women were capable of doing so much more than they were permitted, and it was frustrating! Although some organizations allowed only women members, others accepted men who were also dedicated to the cause.

WE DEMAND THE VOTE.

**South America**

Suffragist organizations also formed links with those in different countries. They exchanged ideas on campaigning and gave each other encouragement. Winning the vote in one country provided momentum for the suffrage campaign in other countries.

**Europe**

DEEDS NOT WORDS

**Asia**

WOMEN'S SUFFRAGE

VOTES FOR WOMEN

**Africa**

VOTES FOR WOMEN

**Australia**

FREEDOM FOR WOMEN

Groups also traveled to other countries to visit fellow suffragists. They gave speeches and took home ideas to progress their cause.

# People Power—Against!

There were organizations to campaign against women's suffrage. Some people—both men and women—thought that women shouldn't get involved in politics.

Opponents considered a woman's temperament to be too delicate and emotional for them to vote sensibly. They worried that voting might make women manly and unfeminine. Some politicians didn't want women to have the vote simply because they didn't think women would vote for them. Women's suffrage was a controversial issue.

⇦ Posters and leaflets tried to persuade people what life would be like if women won the vote.

> **Queen Victoria:**
> "A mad, wicked folly!"

## Not amused

*In Britain, Queen Victoria was adamantly against women's suffrage. Despite the fact that she was a woman who ruled a nation and an empire, she considered women having the vote to be ridiculous—it would mean "forgetting every sense of womanly feeling and propriety."*

## Thousands against

In Great Britain, campaigners produced leaflets and posters ridiculing the suffragists. They had petitions with more than 2,000 signatures agreeing with their views. By 1914, the National League for Opposing Woman Suffrage had 42,000 paying members and thousands more non-paying supporters.

⇦ The National Association Opposed to Woman Suffrage was formed in New York City, in 1911.

⇦ Anti-suffragists thought traditional roles for men and women would be reversed.

⇩ Campaigns by those who were anti-suffrage made fun of women having power. This picture shows a woman having her mouth clamped shut to stop her talking.

# Early Successes

In 1902, Australia became the second country to grant women the vote. A year earlier, the separate colonies of Australia had united to become one nation—and women made sure that their voices were heard.

The 1891 Women's Suffrage Petition in the colony of Victoria had helped to spread the word. The petition was signed by nearly 30,000 women who declared that "women should vote on equal terms with men." Known as the Monster Petition because of its size, the petition was on a roll of fabric so long it took three hours to unroll!

### More equality needed

In 1903, Vida Goldstein, one of the organizers of the Monster Petition, became the first woman to run for the Australian parliament, but was not elected.

AUSTRALIA 1902 VOTE WON

## The European Far North

*Several Nordic countries were next to grant women the right to vote.*

In **Finland**, Baroness Alexandra Gripenberg not only led the campaign for women's suffrage, but also became one of 19 women elected to Parliament in 1906.

FINLAND · 1906 · VOTE WON ·

In **Denmark**, Matilde Bajer and her husband, Fredrik, founded the first organization to campaign for women's rights. Fredrik raised the issue in parliament, and Denmark's new constitution included women's suffrage in 1915.

DENMARK · 1915 · VOTE WON ·

**Norway** granted the vote to wealthy women in 1907 and then extended the vote to all women in 1913, thanks largely to Gina Krog, who campaigned for full equal rights with men—a radical idea at the time.

**Iceland** also granted women the vote in 1915, after Bríet Bjarnhéðinsdóttir and others carried out demonstrations across the country.

NORWAY · 1907 · VOTE WON ·

ICELAND · 1915 · VOTE WON ·

Although the Monster Petition failed in Victoria, other colonies took note. In 1894, the parliament of the neighboring colony of South Australia granted women the vote. They also granted women the right to run for parliament—the first in the world to do so.

White women in Australia won the vote in 1902. However, aboriginal people—who had been living there since long before the white settlers—were not granted the vote until 1962, sixty years after Australia became a nation.

↪ *Women in Victoria, Australia, went door-to-door to collect signatures in support of their petition.*

# Winning in Canada

*In 1896, a group of women, led by Emily Stowe, pretended to be members of the Canadian parliament.*

An amused crowd watched as the women debated whether men should have the right to vote. The crowd laughed, but the mock parliament also made them think—perhaps women should have the vote, as well as men?

Emily wanted to study to be a doctor but was told, "The doors of the University are not open to women." She studied in the United States instead, and then moved back to Canada to practice medicine.

**Nellie McClung:**
"Never underestimate the power of a woman!"

## Nellie McClung

*In 1914, "A Women's Parliament" featured at a theater in the Canadian city of Winnipeg, starring Nellie McClung as the prime minister. Nellie later campaigned for women to be eligible for public office, a move that succeeded in 1929.*

In 1877, Emily founded the Toronto Women's Literary Guild to further education for women. As the campaign for women's rights spread, the club became the Canadian Women's Suffrage Association. They even persuaded the University of Toronto to accept female students. One of the first students was Emily's daughter, Augusta.

Emily paved the way for women in Canada to win the vote in 1916.

# Women of the Russian Revolution

In Russia, women such as Vera Figner took prominent roles alongside Bolshevik (a Russian organization) leader Vladimir Lenin in the struggle against the cruel czars who ruled the country. By 1917, the struggle had become war—the Russian Revolution.

On March 8, 1917, hundreds of thousands of people marked International Women's Day by marching in Russia's capital city, St. Petersburg. They demanded better living conditions and more food for their children.

The old czar was soon replaced by a new government, and women expected the new government to grant them the right to vote. But when the government didn't, more than 40,000 angry women marched again. An aging Vera Figner had pride of place in a motor car.

⇩ The president of the Russian League for Women's Equal Rights, Poliksena Shishkina-lavein was part of the march. She demanded: "We need a clear and official response."

**Poliksena Shishkina-lavein:** "We shall not leave here until we get that response."

All through the night, the women waited, until at last the government agreed. Women had won the vote.

However, even though women had achieved voting rights, when it came to the first elections they were allowed to vote in, things weren't so straightforward. In some villages, men canceled the elections and blocked a woman's path to the voting booth. The fight for voting rights continued.

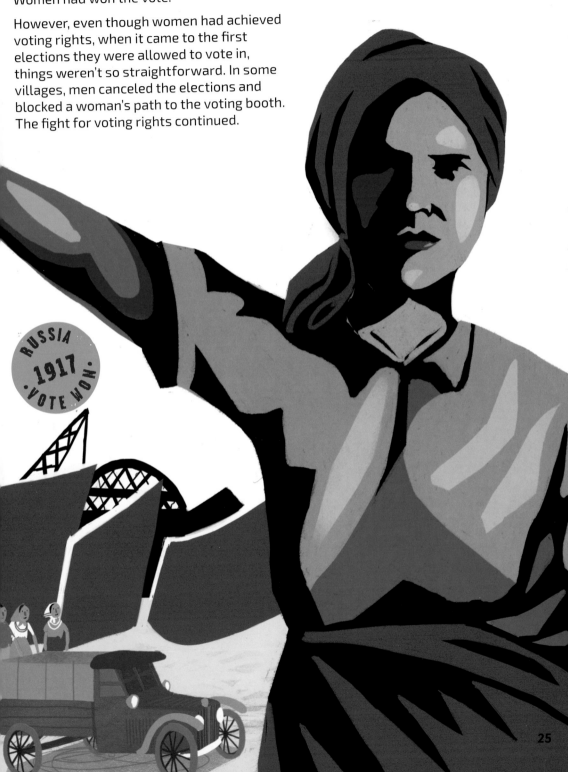

RUSSIA
1917
· VOTE WON ·

# British Suffragists

*In 1865, John Stuart Mill was elected to the British parliament. Although votes for women was part of his election campaign, the issue had been raised earlier by suffragists. Mill was given a petition signed by 1,499 women to present to parliament, asking for women to be given the vote. The answer was no.*

Millicent Garrett Fawcett and her sister Elizabeth campaigned for the vote for more than 50 years. She became president of the National Union of Women's Suffrage Societies (NUWSS), whose membership numbered more than 50,000. Its policy was to be persistent but peaceful. The suffragists presented additional petitions to parliament and held marches and public meetings to spread the word.

But women were getting impatient for the vote . . .

### Women in medicine

*Millicent's sister, Elizabeth Garrett Anderson, became Britain's first female doctor, after first having to fight a bias against women in medicine.*

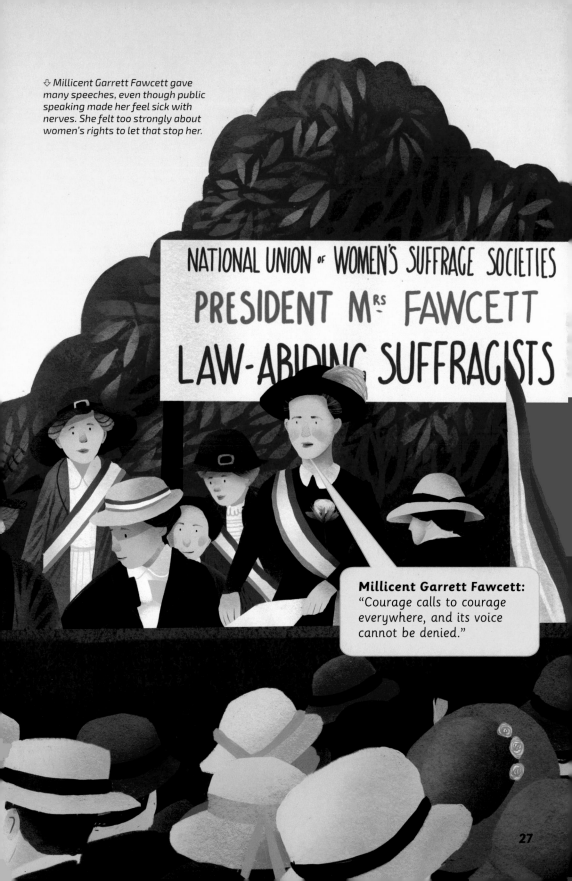

⇩ Millicent Garrett Fawcett gave many speeches, even though public speaking made her feel sick with nerves. She felt too strongly about women's rights to let that stop her.

NATIONAL UNION of WOMEN'S SUFFRAGE SOCIETIES
PRESIDENT Mᴿˢ FAWCETT
LAW-ABIDING SUFFRAGISTS

**Millicent Garrett Fawcett:** "Courage calls to courage everywhere, and its voice cannot be denied."

# British Suffragettes

In Great Britain, in 1903, Emmeline Pankhurst, her daughter, Christabel, and other local women formed the Women's Social and Political Union (WSPU). Only women could be members and they called themselves "suffragettes." Their motto was "Deeds Not Words."

⇧ *Emmeline Pankhurst traveled to the USA to rally support, but met with a lot of resistance.*

The suffragettes held huge rallies and caused uproar at political meetings to bring attention to their cause. As the suffragettes became increasingly frustrated with the government's refusal to grant them the vote, their deeds became more extreme. They chained themselves to railings outside the prime minister's house, smashed windows, set fire to property, slashed paintings in galleries, and blew up mailboxes. Their aim was to bring attention to their cause, although they stopped short of injuring human life.

## Tragedy at the races

*In 1913, suffragette Emily Wilding Davison died after she charged in front of the king's galloping horse at the famous Epsom Derby horse race, in England. She was carrying a distinctive purple, green, and white WSPU scarf.*

The danger involved in these activities meant that suffragettes had to be completely dedicated to the cause. They came from all parts of British society, from wealthy ladies to working-class women earning very little money in factory jobs. They often risked their jobs, their status in society, their friends and families—and their freedom.

⇩ *Suffragettes were forcibly removed from areas and often arrested.*

**Emmeline Pankhurst:**
"Women don't want to be law-breakers, they want to be law-makers!"

⇧ *Emmeline Pankhurst, her daughter Christabel, and Emmeline Pethick-Lawrence (the WSPU's Treasurer) led many suffragette parades.*

# Drastic Actions

Many suffragettes in Britain were arrested, and more than 1,000 went to prison. Sometimes, suffragettes wanted to be arrested so they would appear in the newspaper, bringing more publicity to their campaign. After all, one of their slogans was "Make more noise." Sometimes, the suffragettes protested peacefully but the police arrested them anyway.

⇩ An imprisoned suffragette was put in a cell and made to wear the prison's uniform.

In prison, suffragettes suffered for their just cause. They felt that their actions were a display of political protest, not criminal activity. They went on hunger strike, refusing to eat.

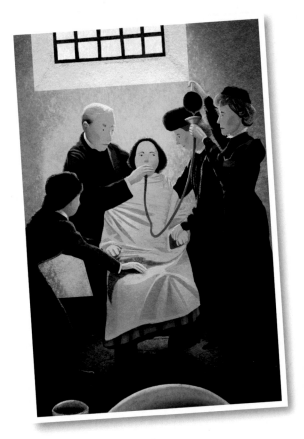

⇨ Prison officials force-fed a suffragette on hunger strike by inserting a tube up her nose or down her throat—an extremely painful procedure.

In 1918, the British government finally granted women the vote—but only if they were aged 30 or over and with certain financial conditions. Women didn't win equal voting rights in Britain until 1928.

⇧ Emmeline Pankhurst and her daughter Christabel had many stretches in prison.

UNITED KINGDOM · 1918 · VOTE WON

## Victory refused

*In 1918, Constance Markievicz (right) became the first woman elected to the British parliament, but she refused to take up her post in protest. In 1919, Nancy Astor became the first woman to serve in parliament as an elected politician.*

# Women in World War I

*World War I (1914—1918) involved many countries across Europe and in other parts of the world. While men from those countries went to fight, women did their jobs at home.*

Before the war, it was a woman's job to look after the home—either their own home, or as a servant. Some women worked in stores and factories. With the outbreak of World War I, the suffragettes and suffragists in Britain turned their attention to helping keep their country running. Women in the United States did the same when their country entered the war in 1917.

During the war, women worked as bus drivers, farmers, firefighters, office workers, police officers, chimney sweeps, grave diggers, and more. Women worked wherever they were needed and proved themselves to be very capable. They became more independent and more confident in the world outside the home.

⇧ In 1915, Marjorie Stinson became the only woman to join the U.S. Aviation Reserve Corps. During the war she trained more than 100 Canadian cadets at the aviation school she founded with her mother and sister in Texas.

⇧ Women manufactured weapons for the war—an extremely dangerous job.

Society became used to seeing women doing work that was previously done by men.

When the war ended and men came back from the battlefront, most women gave up their jobs. However, women had proved themselves in what was considered a man's world. Attitudes toward women were changing.

⇨ *Thousands of women volunteered to help in hospitals at home and overseas.*

⇩ *Some wealthy women who owned cars converted them to ambulances and carried injured people to hospital.*

# After World War I

*With the change in attitudes toward women during and after World War I, more countries in Europe granted the vote to women, including Poland, Germany, and Belgium.*

Aletta Jacobs was a committed advocate of women's rights and equality in the Netherlands. In 1883, she requested a voting ballot for the local election in Amsterdam. She was a tax-paying citizen, so why not? But she was told that "women do not have full citizenship."

Aletta gave speeches in barns in the countryside and at rallies in the cities. The Dutch suffragists also met personally with politicians to raise the issue in parliament. Aletta became a leading member of the International Woman Suffrage Alliance and exchanged ideas with other suffragists. Even after the Netherlands granted women the vote in 1919, she traveled the world publicizing the cause of women's suffrage.

**Aletta Jacobs:**
"From my sixth year onwards I have always stated with the utmost clarity that I wanted to become a doctor. Never did the thought come to me that this would be difficult for a girl."

### Permission to study

*In 1879, Aletta became the first female doctor in the Netherlands, but only after she wrote a letter to the Dutch prime minister asking special permission for a place to study medicine at a university.*

⇩ Dutch suffragists sailed along the canals in decorated barges to spread their campaign for the vote.

POLAND
·1918·
VOTE WON

GERMANY
·1918·
VOTE WON

BELGIUM
·1919·
VOTE WON

VOTES FOR WOMEN

NETHERLANDS
·1919·
VOTE WON

# Suffrage in the U.S.

By the early 1900s, a new generation of suffragists had taken over the campaign in the United States, led by Carrie Chapman Catt. Carrie also founded the International Woman Suffrage Alliance to stay in touch with organizations in different countries.

Meanwhile, Alice Paul, Lucy Burns, and Harriet Stanton Blatch (daughter of Elizabeth Cady Stanton) traveled to England to campaign with the Pankhursts. The British suffragettes gave them ideas on how to organize protest actions that would attract maximum attention.

They organized more marches and demonstrations. Supporters cheered them on, but opponents jeered and ripped down their banners. The women were often arrested and taken to prison, where some went on hunger strike. Like the British suffragettes, they were also force fed.

↓ A group of suffragists known as the "Silent Sentinels" demonstrated outside the White House every day (except Sundays) for two and a half years.

### Equal Rights Amendment

*In 1923, Alice Paul drafted the Equal Rights Amendment, a document guaranteeing women the same rights as men. As of 2018, the Equal Rights Amendment has not been ratified by enough states for passage.*

⇩ In the U.S., parades for women's suffrage were at first met with interest and sympathy, but attitudes quickly changed.

At last, in 1919, Congress passed the 19th Amendment to the Constitution. It took another year for enough states to ratify, or approve, the Amendment in order for it to become law in 1920—a full 72 years after the first Woman's Rights Convention in Seneca Falls. The 19th Amendment is sometimes called the "Susan B. Anthony Amendment!"

UNITED STATES · 1920 · VOTE WON

# More Global Success

The campaign for women's suffrage was spreading around the world—and women were winning the vote in more and more countries . . .

ECUADOR 1929 VOTE WON

⇧ When Mathilde Hidalgo de Procel applied to university, officials initially told her that she should look after her home and family.

## Ecuador

Mathilde Hidalgo de Procel became the first girl to graduate from secondary school in the South American country of Ecuador. She'd had to get special permission to attend and was treated like an outcast. Mathilde continued her education at a university and became the first female doctor in Ecuador.

In 1924, Mathilde registered to vote. When the State Council objected, she argued that she met all of the requirements for voters in Ecuador. She was a citizen, was over the age of 21, and could read and write. The State Council agreed, and Mathilde became the first woman to vote in Ecuador. In 1929, Ecuador became the first country in South America to grant women the vote.

## Support in powerful places

*First lady Florence Harding was the wife of U.S. President Warren G Harding. In 1922, she met a group of women from the Philippines who had traveled to Washington, D.C. They wanted support in their fight for their country's independence.*

# Philippines

War in the early 1900s had led to widespread malnutrition in the Philippines. Concepción Felix was a Filipino lawyer who worked to help women and children. She founded the Feminist Association of the Philippines and also helped establish a program to improve nutrition for mothers and babies.

The Philippine Assembly debated the first suffrage bill in 1907, but it failed. Encouraged by American suffragist Carrie Chapman Catt, Concepción began working with journalist Pura Villanueva to campaign for women's suffrage. Slowly, the movement grew.

In 1937, the government promised to grant women the vote if more than 300,000 women were in favor. In fact, 447,725 women voted for suffrage. It was a landslide victory!

PHILIPPINES
1937
·VOTE WON·

⇨ *Former beauty queen Pura Villanueva wrote a newspaper column campaigning for women's suffrage.*

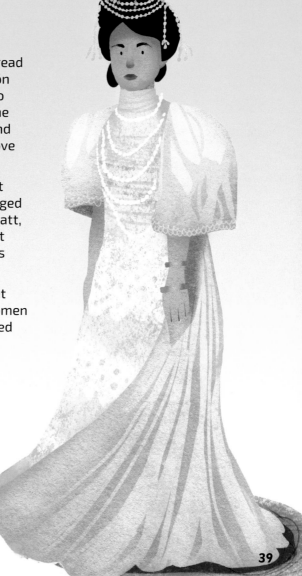

# Women in World War II

*When war yet again caused turmoil across the world, women once more stepped in to do whatever work was required. As in World War I, women took over traditional men's jobs.*

During World War II (1939—1945), women were encouraged to help in the war effort directly. In Great Britain, for example, women took on duties such as providing aid to bombing victims, monitoring enemy aircraft, driving military vehicles, and deciphering enemy codes. Some women proved themselves to be courageous secret agents.

### Women in Nazi Germany

*The Nazi government believed that a woman's place was in the home. But during World War II, they needed women to work on farms and in factories to help keep the country running.*

⇧ *Women who became secret agents during the war risked their lives to obtain information that would help their country.*

⇧⇩ Photographs and posters show the vital work women were undertaking.

During World War II, the general view of women changed. Their determination, intelligence, and spirit earned the respect of the general public. But after the war, women were no longer needed to do what were considered men's jobs. Most women returned to their traditional role of taking care of the family and home. However, women had gained new respect that strengthened the call to women's suffrage around the world.

# Opposite Sides of the World

*Although women now had the vote in many places, the fight continued. They would not give up until they had won the vote in every country.*

## France

For a long time, women in France campaigned for suffrage with little success. In the 1880s, Hubertine Auclert attempted to vote, refused to pay taxes, and even ran for public office.

None of her tactics worked, but they paved the way for future campaigners, such as Madeleine Pelletier, who overcame poverty to become a doctor, and wealthy Marguerite Durand, who paraded her pet lioness around Paris to gain publicity for women's suffrage. Women in France finally won the vote in 1944.

⇧ Hubertine Auclert was an actress and passionate suffragist. She created her own feminist daily newspaper.

FRANCE 1944 · VOTE WON

# Japan

Traditional Japanese custom held that women should walk behind men, and they certainly weren't permitted to participate in politics. Fusae Ichikawa rebelled against these old customs. She traveled to the USA, where she was inspired by suffragists. Fusae returned to Japan in 1924 and founded the Women's Suffrage League of Japan. Slowly, she managed to gain more rights for women, but the vote still seemed out of reach.

After World War II, American officials temporarily took charge of Japan, and Fusae brought the issue of women's suffrage to their attention. In December 1945, women finally won the vote. In 1946, more than two-thirds of Japanese women voted in the national election, and 39 women were elected to public office.

⇧ Fusae was elected to parliament in 1953 and served for many years.

JAPAN
1945
·VOTE WON·

# Poet and Protester

Since 1858, Great Britain had ruled India, but the people of India wanted independence. Known as "The Nightingale of India," Sarojini Naidu was a famous poet and a key campaigner for equality and independence.

### The Nightingale of India

*Sarojini is known for her beautiful poetry, including verses such as "Past and Future," "Indian Love Song," and "To My Children." Her birthday is celebrated in India as Women's Day.*

Along with many others, Sarojini was a passionate campaigner for an independent India. Campaigners for independence are called nationalists. She was the first female president of the Indian National Congress, but her protests against British rule later resulted in time in prison.

Sarojini also campaigned for Indian women to have equal rights—including the right to vote. She traveled around the country campaigning for women's suffrage.

⇨ *The fight for independence was led by Mahatma Gandhi (center with staff).*

Along with British suffragist Annie Besant, who had moved from Britain to India, Sarojini set up the Indian Women's Association and published a feminist news magazine. Together, they traveled to London to raise the issue of women's suffrage with British politicians.

Meanwhile, the Indian National Congress promised that women would have the vote once the country became independent. In 1947, India finally became free and women were able to vote. Sarojini was elected governor of the province that is now Uttar Pradesh.

⬦ Annie Besant (right) wrote to British newspapers arguing the case for women's suffrage, in India.

INDIA
1947
·VOTE WON·

# From Poverty to Power

*In Argentina, Julieta Lanteri-Renshaw was the first campaigner for women's suffrage. She founded the National Feminist Union, applied to vote, ran for public office, and even held a mock election in 1920—all without success.*

Then, in 1946, Maria Eva Durate de Perón, known as Eva, became first lady of Argentina. Eva came from a poor family. Her mother worked many different jobs to feed Eva and her sisters. She influenced her husband, President Juan Perón, to improve conditions for the poor and to support women's rights.

When her husband became president, she persuaded his opponents in parliament to agree to a women's suffrage bill, even threatening to live in the Congress building until women won the vote. In 1947, thousands of people celebrated in the streets when the women's suffrage bill became law. The first Argentine election in which women took part occurred in 1951.

⇩ *Eva Perón's rise to power became famous around the world.*

⇨ *Thousands of women attended rallies to listen to Eva Perón speak.*

ARGENTINA · 1947 · VOTE WON ·

46

In the following years, women's suffrage became law in countries throughout South and Central America and in the Caribbean—including countries such as Venezuela, Suriname, Chile, Costa Rica, Barbados, Haiti, and more. Women across the region were winning the vote!

⇧ Protests in Chile took place outside government buildings.

Eva Perón:
"I am my own woman!"

# The Lioness of Lasabi

*During the 1940s and 1950s, women's suffrage spread across Africa. The country of South Africa had already granted limited suffrage to women in 1930, but now women were winning the vote in other countries, such as Cameroon, Liberia, Ethiopia, Ghana, and Senegal.*

Doria Shafik led a new generation of women's suffrage campaigners in Egypt. Doria published a magazine promoting women's rights, and in 1951, she led 1,500 women in a protest at the Egyptian parliament to demand the vote. She later went on hunger strike. Her protests and publications helped Egyptian women win the vote in 1956.

Nigerian campaigner Funmilayo Ransome-Kuti founded the first organization in what became the Federation of Nigerian Women's Societies. When a woman working at the local market asked Funmilayo to teach her to read, Funmilayo began campaigning to improve conditions for poor women. She led a series of protests against laws that were unfair to women.

Funmilayo was famous for her courage and was called the "Lioness of Lasabi" and the "Mother of Africa." Nigeria granted limited voting rights to women in 1958, with full suffrage in 1976.

## Further education

*Funmilayo was a student at the Abeokuta Grammar School in Nigeria. She also studied in Great Britain. Later, she became a teacher at her school back in Nigeria.*

⇩ Funmilayo once grabbed a traditional "oro" stick that symbolized a man's power, holding it above her head to show that women could have power, too.

EGYPT
· 1956 ·
· VOTE WON ·

NIGERIA
1958
· VOTE WON ·

# Recent Struggles

*Women in some Arab nations have had to fight especially hard to win the vote, and it has taken a long time. Suffragists in countries such as Kuwait, Qatar, and the United Arab Emirates have relied on the modern technology of cell phones, computers, and social media to spread the word about women's rights.*

In 2005, Rola Dashti of Kuwait used social media to organize a peaceful demonstration outside the country's parliament building. Women won the right to vote in that same year, and Rola was the first woman to register.

Women in Saudi Arabia won the right to vote in 2015. Yet sadly, voter turnout among women was low. Registering to vote was not made easy for women. Some couldn't register because they didn't have the correct documentation, others felt pressure not to register. Still others simply couldn't get to the registration office because they needed a male relative to take them. Nevertheless, winning the right to vote was a big step forward and hopefully more rights will follow.

⇧ *In the 2009 elections, Rola Dashti was among four women who became Kuwait's first female members of parliament.*

## Further rights

*In 2018, women in Saudi Arabia were finally allowed to drive cars. Previously, it had been illegal for a woman to drive a car. Saudi feminists continue to campaign for more rights for women.*

KUWAIT
2005
· VOTE WON ·

SAUDI ARABIA
2015
· VOTE WON ·

# Votes for Women!

Suffragists publicized their cause with slogans and quotes that were brief and easy to remember. Today, such slogans and quotes are often called "sound bites." They're short, thought provoking, and get straight to the point—plus they're often very witty.

"Equal justice for men and women."
**Emmeline Pankhurst**

"Men, their rights and nothing more; women, their rights and nothing less."
**Susan B Anthony**

# DARE TO BE FREE

"How long must a woman wait for liberty?"
**Inez Milholland, U.S. suffrage campaigner**

"The best protection a woman can have is courage."
**Millicent Garrett Fawcett**

# INDEPENDENCE IS HAPPINESS

"We are tired of having a 'sphere' doled out to us, and of being told that anything outside that sphere is 'unwomanly.'"
**Kate Sheppard**

# NO VOTE, NO TAX

# BE RIGHT AND PERSIST

"No duties without rights; no rights without duties."
**French Women's Suffrage Society**

"It is only simple justice that women demand."
**Christabel Pankhurst**

"It is unthinkable that a national government which represents women should ignore the issue of the right of all women to political freedom."
**Lucy Burns**

# JUSTICE NOT PRIVILEGE

# The Fight for Women's Rights

Heraus mit dem Frauenwahlrecht
**FRAUEN-TAG**
8. MÄRZ 1914

Sonntag den 8. März 1914 nachmittags 3 Uhr stattfindend

**9 öffentl. Frauen-Versammlungen**

*Winning the right to vote was a major victory for women. Voting finally gave women a say because it meant that when women voiced their concerns, politicians had to pay attention if they wanted women to vote for them.*

In 1966, a group of American feminists founded the National Organization for Women (NOW) to campaign for a fully equal partnership between the sexes. It was the era of women's liberation. Liberation means freedom, and the women's lib movement gave women around the world a new sense of freedom, with greater opportunity and more power to make decisions over their own lives. Women were making progress, but they were a long way from reaching full equality with men.

⇧ *Since 1911, International Women's Day (March 8) has been celebrated around the world to recognize women's achievements and call for greater equality.*

⇨ *In 1968, women workers at a British factory demanded the same pay as the men workers who did the same job. The women went on strike and refused to work until the company agreed.*

## World Leaders

*With the vote, women also started running for political office. Some were elected to govern their countries. But men still far outnumbered women in politics. These are some female leaders of the late 20th century.*

**Margaret Thatcher**
Prime Minister of the United Kingdom
(1979—1990)

**Benazir Bhutto**
Prime Minister of Pakistan
(1988—1990 and 1993—1996)

## Battle of the Sexes

*When tennis player Bobby Riggs declared in 1973 that he could beat any female player, Billie Jean King proved him wrong in a famous match known as the "Battle of the Sexes." Billie Jean's victory showed that women were just as capable as men.*

**Indira Gandhi**
Prime Minister of India (1966—1977 and 1980—1984)

**Corazon Aquino**
President of the Philippines (1986—1992)

# Toward Equality

*These days, most women have more choices and opportunities than ever before. They can go to college and have careers. They can become world leaders or astronauts, athletes, or business people.*

But even now, women are still not always treated equally to men. They may not receive equal pay and equal opportunities in areas such as jobs and education. Women need freedom to make decisions for themselves. They need to feel safe and respected. There's a long way to go before men and women have equal rights everywhere in the world—but winning the vote was a big step forward.

### Girls and School

*While still a schoolgirl, Malala Yousafzai risked her life to campaign for girls to have the right to go to school. More than 130 million girls around the world still do not have that opportunity. The Malala Fund campaigns for girls everywhere to have an education.*

EQUAL RIGHTS

RI

W

⇦ Thousands of women marched through Istanbul, Turkey, on International Women's Day in 2014.

### The "Glass Ceiling"

Women still often get paid less than men for doing the same job. While some women have managed to reach the top of their chosen career, sexism known as the "glass ceiling" still prevents many others from achieving their potential.

QUALI
NOW

EQUALITY
FOR
WOMEN

RIGHTS
FOR
WOMEN

# Gender Equality and You

*These days, instead of saying "women's rights," the term "gender equality" is often used. Along with campaigning for rights for women, this also means supporting rights for men.*

Traditional gender roles no longer apply. For example, now men can look after their children and home, and women can go out to work. Gender equality means everyone can do what's right for them as individuals, regardless of gender.

Here are some ideas on how you can stand up for gender equality. The first idea is easy: just be yourself. Everyone is an individual, and there's no particular way that a girl or a boy is supposed to act.

*Do what you like doing. You don't have to pay attention to traditional gender stereotypes. How about playing soccer or ballet dancing? They're both fun, and it doesn't matter if you're a girl or a boy.*

### He for She

*Actress Emma Watson launched the United Nations "He for She" project to inspire everyone to stand up for gender equality. Among those who have committed to take action for gender equality are leaders of governments, businesses, and universities.*

**HeForShe**
UN Women Solidarity Movement for Gender Equality

Think about gender equality at school. Are girls and boys treated equally? Does everyone get a fair chance in P.E. and on sports teams? Do you discuss the achievements of both men and women in your classes?

Talk to your teacher or your student council if you notice that girls and boys are not being treated equally at school. You could even form a club to discuss equal rights.

What job do you want to do when you grow up? You're lucky that you live in a time when the job you do doesn't depend on whether you are a man or a woman.

Read books and watch movies starring "sheroes" (girls and women) as well as heroes!

No matter what your gender, you have the right to respect. Call out language or behavior that is disrespectful to yourself or others. And remember to give respect to others!

NOT >

NOT <

BUT =

# Hall of Fame

Although women are able to vote in the majority of countries around the world, their fight for equality continues. Here are some female pioneers who have made a difference.

**Abigail Adams (1744—1818)** *was wife and mother to two U.S. presidents. She voiced strong opinions to her husband about women's rights and female education.*

**Mary Wollstonecraft (1759—1797)** *is considered a leading feminist and wrote revolutionary literature on why women should be given the same education as men.*

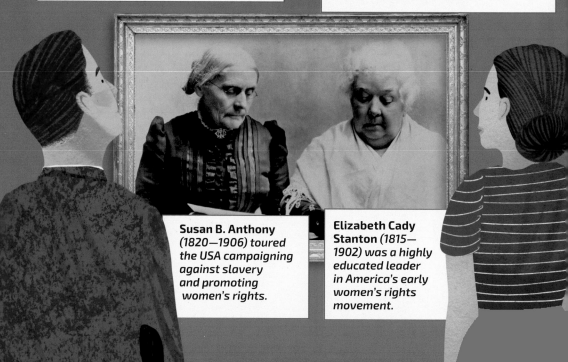

**Susan B. Anthony (1820—1906)** *toured the USA campaigning against slavery and promoting women's rights.*

**Elizabeth Cady Stanton (1815—1902)** *was a highly educated leader in America's early women's rights movement.*

**Kate Sheppard** (1847—1934) was a key figure for women's suffrage in New Zealand—the first country to allow women the right to vote, in 1893.

**Emmeline Pankhurst** (1858—1928) was leader of the British suffragettes, whose protests involved marches and hunger strikes.

**Millicent Garrett Fawcett** (1846—1929) led Britain's largest nonviolent suffrage organization, the NUWSS.

**Malala Yousafzai** (1997—) is the youngest person to have received the Nobel Peace Prize. She campaigns for peace, education, and equality, for every child.

# Glossary

**Campaign** A series of organized actions that come together to achieve a goal. Women campaigned for the right to vote.

**Candidate** A person who takes part in an election for a position in public office. Citizens vote in elections for their favorite candidate to win.

**Constitution** The rules and laws that outline how some countries are run. Every citizen of that country must live by the laws of their country's constitution.

**Czar** A former head of the Russian monarchy and leader of Russia. Russia was ruled by the monarchy until November 1917 when the last czar abdicated (gave up his leadership).

**Election** A contest where candidates compete for a position into public office. Citizens vote for a candidate, and the one who wins is elected into that position.

**Equality** The idea that every person in society deserves to have equal rights and opportunities, no matter their gender, race, religion, ability, or identity.

**Feminism** The idea that women should have the same rights and opportunities as men. Someone who believes in or campaigns for feminism is called a feminist.

**Glass ceiling** An invisible barrier, made up of laws and attitudes that stop women from achieving the same opportunities as men.

**Government** A group of elected officials who decide how a country is run

**Member of Parliament (MP)** A person who is elected to parliament to vote on and help to make laws on behalf of the citizens who elected them.

**Nationalism** The idea that a countr should look after its own citizens and businesses first before considering the interests of other countries.

**Nazi Party** The political party that controlled Germany from 1933 unt 1945 when World War II ended.

**Parliament** A group of electe officials who come together to discuss, make, and vote on issues and laws.

**Petition** A list of signatures from people who support an idea and want it put in place. Sometimes petitions are taken to the government to show that many people want an idea to be made into law.

**Protest** Actions that show a person or group of people do not support something. People may go on protest marches to show they don't support a proposed idea or a law that has been passed.

**Public office** A position of power or service where a person has a responsibility to represent and listen to citizens. Presidents and prime minsters hold public offices, as well as court judges.

**Sexism** Being treated unfairly because of your gender. Many people who believe in equality fight against sexism.

**Suffrage** The right to vote in elections. Before women started campaigning, only men had suffrage.

**Suffragette** A woman who campaigned for the right to vote. Suffragettes held rallies, chained themselves to railings, and took part in non-peaceful protests to draw attention to their cause.

**Suffragist** A person who supported women's right to suffrage and protested peacefully. Many men and women were suffragists.

# *Index*

**A**
aboriginal people 21
Adams, Abigail 10, 60
Africa 48–49
Anderson, Elizabeth Garrett 26
Anthony, Susan B. 12, 52, 60
Arab nations 50
Argentina 46
Astor, Nancy 31
Auclert, Hubertine 42
Australia 20, 21

**B C**
Bajer, Matilde 21
Belgium 34
Besant, Annie 45
Bjarnhéðinsdóttir, Bríet 21
Bloomer, Amelia 13
Britain 18, 26–31, 36, 40
Canada 22–23
Catt, Carrie Chapman 36, 39
Chile 47

**D E F**
Dashti, Rola 50
Davison, Emily Wilding 28
Denmark 21
Ecuador 38
education 10, 14, 23, 38, 49, 56
Egypt 48
Equal Rights Amendment 36
equal rights struggle 10, 12, 21, 36, 54, 56
Fawcett, Millicent Garrett 26, 27, 52, 61
Felix, Concepción 39
feminism 14
Figner, Vera 24
Finland 21
France 11, 42

**G H**
gender equality 58–59
Germany 34, 40

glass ceiling 57
Goldstein, Vida 20
Gripenberg, Baroness Alexandra 21
Hidalgo de Procel, Mathilde 38

**I J K**
Iceland 21
Ichikawa, Fusae 43
importance of having the vote 8
imprisonment 30–31, 36, 44
India 44–45
International Women's Day 54
Jacobs, Aletta 34
Japan 43
King, Billie Jean 55
Krog, Gina 21
Kuwait 50

**L M**
Lanteri-Renshaw, Dr Julieta 46
McClung, Nellie 22
male supporters 8, 12, 16, 21, 26
Maori women 7
Markievicz, Constance 31
medicine, women in 15, 22, 26, 34, 38, 42
Mill, Harriet 26
Mill, John Stuart 26
Mott, Lucretia Coffin 121

**N O P**
Naidu, Sarojini 44–45
Netherlands 34
New Zealand 6–7
Nigeria 48–49
Norway 21
opponents of women's suffrage 18–19

Pankhurst, Emmeline 28, 29, 31, 52, 61
Paul, Alice 36, 43
Perón, Eva 46
Philippines 39
Poland 34
political office, women in 15, 20, 21, 22, 31, 43, 44, 45, 50, 54–55
protest actions 8, 28–29, 36

**R S T**
Ransome-Kuti, Funmilayo 48–49
Russia 24–25
Saudi Arabia 50
Seneca Falls conventions 12–13, 14
Shafik, Doria 48
Sheppard, Kate 6–7, 53, 61
"sound bites" 52–53
South and Central America 46–47
Stanton, Elizabeth Cady 12, 60
Stinson, Marjorie 32
Stone, Lucy 13
Stowe, Emily 22–23
suffragettes 28–29, 30–31, 36, 61
suffragists 8, 12, 16–17, 26, 35, 36, 52
Truth, Sojourner 13

**U V W**
United States 10, 12–15, 19, 28, 32, 36–37, 54
Victoria, Queen 18
Walker, Dr Mary Edwards 15
war work 32–33, 40–41
Wollstonecraft, Mary 11, 60
Woodhull, Victoria 15
World War I and II 32–33, 40–41
Yousafzai, Malala 56, 61